A WARM AND SNC

A WARM AND SNOUTING THING

By Ramona Herdman

THE EMMA PRESS

THE EMMA PRESS

First published in the UK in 2019 by the Emma Press Ltd

Poems copyright © Ramona Herdman 2019

Edited by Richard O'Brien
Typeset by Emma Wright

ISBN 978-1-912915-29-3

A CIP catalogue record of this book
is available from the British Library.

Printed and bound in the UK
by Oxuniprint Ltd, Oxford.

The Emma Press
theemmapress.com
hello@theemmapress.com
Birmingham, UK

CONTENTS

He sits slightly too close and we don't look at each other

I thought it had gone – my sex-sense,
the skin-thrum awareness when you feel
through your clothes sex's presence.
But the nerves all down my left side sizzle.
I can feel him through three inches of air.
I'm humming with it. Not at all like
an electric shock. Perhaps a bit
like your naked tongue about to lick
a battery. Quite like sudden sun
through a window – dazzling one eye.
Almost the same as standing stock-still
as the bonfire's heat advances,
feeling its breath start to hurt your face
as you stare back, smoke in your throat.

Jill had two ponies

One skewbald, one black, I think. Gymkhanas.
Rosettes. Dressage. Cross-country courses.
Near-crises averted. Jill learnt about kindness.

Tackle and bridle and saddle-soap
and saddle-sores. Horseboxes and riding boots.
The unmentioned absence of parents.

The way a life can focus on just one
crystal-ball intensity. No need to mention shitting
or the boring businesses of teeth-cleaning, sleeping.

We know Jill has a roof over her head
and doesn't need to know about earning a living,
about periods or the morning-after pill. She doesn't

daydream about no-good boys fighting, physically
fighting over her, heavy wet imagined
slap of a punch in the face, lip splitting on teeth.

The best bits are when she finds forest rides,
the trees parting mistily. Dew in the grass.
Not gothic fairytale forests, but soft

deciduous English woodlands. Sun through
the branches in patches and flutes. Bracken.
Puddles copper-warm. Birdsong. The delayed

patter of rain from the canopy. Going in
and in and in. No horizon. Just more
delicious corners. Mosses and lichens.

No Better Than She Should Be Red

This summer my reward

for hanging out the washing
bringing in the washing
rushing out to rescue from the rain the washing

slatternly   bra-less   in pajamas
on scarlet tip-toe

is alpine strawberries –

the garden tapestried
with shock-sweet little nippled sherbet candies
slug-beloved

vigorous   sprawling   decadent   shameless.

Nudes

That was the house I was naked in.
Eight, nine? Summer-comfortable just in skin,
butter baby, unselfconscious, playing
in the stained glass shadows on the parquet,
wooden bricks sticking to my tummy.
My parents didn't like it. They said
I could be seen from outside. Imagine
me: a little fat lamp at the window.

Next house, it was my dad: mid-argument,
pre-divorce, he'd strip off. He did it once
in front of my mum's friends, making a point,
his sad body like something at the zoo.

Ferns

for Adam

When I said you were like ferns
it wasn't sex I was thinking of, but shade
and green. Soft deep unshowiness and quiet.
In any ruckus, your calm face smiling.
But there's no denying the spring in them,
the slow force of their unfurl. It's sex,

male sex, not crosiers like they say – that nest
of curls in the cool limestone corner of shade
I step down into. Forest-whispering ferns,
dinosaur-high. Insects' serious dancing
above the sunken path. Cool wet plant-sex
of swamped millennia. It's been years

and there's no need for bouquets or rose-gardens.
Remember crawling through bracken?
Foxes in a hole, dried-leaf scratch in the shade
of summer's growth. Let's plant a garden of ferns
in the lee of our house. Moss and water.
As many greens as there are in sex.

Sixteen

Lying on the beach in my first bikini
in a line of women like seals,
I listened to her tell my mother she grew
her armpit hair because her husband liked it.
Sweat and seaweed. Bare feet on the metal stairs.

That evening she walked me over the fields to Dark Trees.
The copse of cypresses like a room in the night,
glow-worms green as UFOs.
She told me what she worried for her sons.
When we got back, the whole holiday household
was out looking for us.

Another day I was gently let off for sneaking away
a book of bondage erotica they'd been passing round –
the humiliation of my parents explaining,
sitting either side of me,
that sex wouldn't be like that.

And I've never asked if my mother knew,
when she invited her, she was my father's lover.
The two of them dead now.

And it was perhaps a different summer
that old man who'd been my mum's first boyfriend
(lithe fisherboy, he must have been)
left a carrier bag hung on our front door,
clicking and shifting – two huge crabs, rough as roof-tiles.
I hid in the basement while she boiled them alive,
her face young with steam, jewels in her hair.

Shave

The backs of men's necks
queue on the Tube.
Hot breath and the mustn't
of reaching to touch. Such
a little inch of shared air
to transgress. Sticky dress
and long haul home to owned skin.

When I was eighteen,
my lover asked me to stand over him
with little buzzing clippers, to stroke
the hair off with their insect mouth.
I kissed all up that new tickle
of conquered skull, triumphant.
My thumb the first to smooth across, enjoy
the bite of new-cut hair.

Another summer, older,
and it's my father asking.
Widower, too ill to go out.
Such uncomfortable trespass,
shudder and prickle,
to walk the clippers the way his second wife did,
cut paths over his small grey head –
then holster them in the leatherette case
and put them away
in the too-tidy bathroom
of his last house.

There will always be another summer.
This one, both of us
in this dappled, dazzling bath,
I rest one heel
                then the other
on your shoulder, lean back
and trust your razor
down my leg, nuzzling
the unseen back of my knee.

Daphne

It was a red-brick university.
A bit of the classics, a bit of Marlowe:
> *but that was in another country,*
> *And besides, the wench is dead.*

Gods as swans, as stags;
naiads ever-replenishing like laughing rain.
We could spot a phallic symbol a mile off.
All of us on the pill, no question,
and on the prowl.
And mostly unsuccessful.

I think perhaps it was my ugliness that saved me.
Looking back, I was lucky –
night after night wide-eyed off my face through the city
wearing nothing but glitter, heels,
a vintage satin slip
with straps that snapped on the dancefloor
forever needing knotting back up.

But then they say
> any woman can get laid anytime she wants
> if she lowers her standards enough,
> that you can't blame wild dogs
> for attacking raw meat left in the road,
> that you should wear flats
> so you can run away.

O nights I half-remember!
Old men buying us trebles.
Telling a boy of my really clear memory
of holding someone's hand the night before

and him saying, *That was me.*
Nights I insisted on keeping my knickers on
or changed my mind buck-naked.
Thanks be to the men, to the world that let me.

But Daphne was beautiful.
We half-hated her for it.
I wonder now if some bad fairy
leant over her in envy once upon a time, said,
Yes, be beautiful. Be set apart.
Be water in the air. Be currency.
Be pawed. Be owned.
Be set apart from women. Be unsafe.

She kept on soft as the flow of water
till we forgot her face and liked her.
Shocked us like the dazzle of sun on sea
when Saturday night dolled-up – but we forgave her.
My mum called her The Alpha Female.

Water on a concrete campus. She shone.
She could've had anyone.
You know what they say
         you don't want what you can get.

Next to her, we were stick women.
From the Dean down, she got a reaction.
Lecturers ludicrous.
She almost gave in to the one
who'd been writing her essays.
He couldn't believe his luck –
then ever after was scrabbled away with rage
that she froze last minute, said no.

How we howled when he published his novel about it,
him the hero, shining Apollo.

We were glad.
Hadn't wanted his hot old hands on her.
Wanted her kept clear like the moon on water.
We sat on her bed and laughed as she packed to go home.
Never guessed she wouldn't come back.

Fifteen years on, I meet her on Facebook,
giving nothing away. No relationship status.
A fine-looking woman for her age.
Great posture. Nothing like water.
More like a broad tree that owns
its own space, holds its fill of air.

Shaped

ticked
sleek   choices
the   of kempt
love   women's
I   eyebrows

swoosh and
badgery   thickening of other women's
the   eyebrows, silently luscious, just as
love   conscious, a surging flourish, like
I   brambled hedgerow tangle

and that's before   moustaches
even getting   who pet their
onto the women

or those who
allow
the
a   odd
like   spell   hair
chin   to
their   curl
under

I'll never have a child to bring to this beach

My mother phones to say
walking's got difficult so she's decided to stop.
My heart clutches

but fair enough. She has tried the world
and if she wants to say *Fuck it,*
who am I to know better?

Her own mother can't string
much together anymore,
but knows enough to say

You know Ramona
won't look after you when you're old.
Meanly. Rightly.

She blames my mother
for bringing me up to think
I'm too good for this world.

Buttoned

It was the buttons, luscious as sex,
mother-of-pearling down her back.
It was the run of buttons made you want to look
under and undo them with a jade-handled buttonhook.
She sat laced-in proper, solid as a swan,
but looked over her shoulder with the old come-on.
She'd button herself early against the morning mist
and go out all demurely to chase a kiss.
She was perverse as purity, all buttoned-up and bitter.
As men walked by she cast her eye down amongst the litter.
She held her breath all morning, until her flesh was patterned
in preparation for the hour that she'd come unbuttoned.

Marilyn

How can we blame you for blurring life
with alcohol and barbiturates,
when we all want to rub our faces blind
on your soft stomach, your breasts,

have you breathe sad bourbon fumes
into our mouths, sing a song,
sling a quip, then tap a tune
in perfect syncopation?

You were born with one bit of luck (your looks)
and you used it like a mountain –
years of work, snow-blindness, crampon hooks,
and the whole of your life climbing.

They tell your marriages like a fairy tale –
the boy next door, the sports star,
the sensitive intellectual –
like counting to three means happy ever after.

Holly Golightly was written for you:
wild animal, living on change
for the restroom. *The mean reds, the blues.*
Poor slob, poor cat with no name.

Marilyn, you're the ghost of trying.
Snowfield face and sequined sheath.
Work and wanting and wanting in that white-out smile.
You make me hold my breath.

I watch you shimmy, in clothes too tight to walk in –
jello on springs, kissing Hitler – in heels that hurt,
thigh sliding round thigh, down the platform.
Hassled by steam and a wah-wah tune. Perfect.

Comeuppance

The girls walk down the train aisle in glittery eyeshadow
and vest tops in April. The creepy old men are watching them

and they like it. There is an aura of self-consciousness
around them like dazzle off a pool at twilight, thick perfume.

They could be fourteen. Or sixteen. How could we not
look up from our laptops? We in our suits or cardigans.

I want to fight the man who makes an *ouch* face to himself
watching their departing bottoms. As if it was funny.

I have a hurt in my stomach for it. As if I were
someone's mother. I want to fight off the world for them.

And I remember the sudden novelty
of making adult men feel something.

Of stealing some of their power. Making a ripple
in the world. I remember my mum asking if the boys

wouldn't put their hands up a skirt that short:
it had never occurred to me that anyone could

without my say-so.
                                    I want to tell them

they have every right to bare their lovely bare arms,
their ideal shoulders (no matter how cold it is out).

Every right to stretch our credulity as we're reminded
how glorious an ordinary girl can be,

how bodies are meant to be, as my mum says.
But also to say, *In this world as it is, put on armour.*

Be aware of men's power, even as you make them feel things.
Even as you draw them unstoppably after you.

The world is not as it should be, my loves.
Enjoy it.

Bless email and bless boredom and bless

our managers' occupied disinterest
and bless the fat in the public sector
that there was then. Bless our innocence

and bless the flex in our young marriages.
Bless being seated twenty steps apart and at
an angle so there was no risk of eye

snagging eye. Oh, and bless language for its
ambiguity. Bless not-quite invitations
not quite enough to evidence a disciplinary

and bless nine-to-five endlessness and bless
not taking joint tea-breaks, not walking
to the shops at lunch together, not

being like the office joke adulterers,
who'd hump before work in the carpark, hold hands
at staff dos. Bless going home to our lives.

But mostly bless that ongoing precise
and dancing mental drafting
while dealing with spreadsheets,

purchase orders and all the other emails.
Bless the heart's ping
when one arrived with your name next to it.

Bless that summer-breathed continuation
of back of the class subdued naughtiness.
And bless us for stopping it.

This is just to say

(after William Carlos Williams)

I don't want to
fuck you
delicious
forgive me

I want
to share cigarettes
after years
not smoking

then back off
to our marriages
so cool
and so sweet

Precipitation

I watch snow melt into the reservoir,
with nothing to say to my ill brother.
Twenty years ago, mud-naïve, we struggled
my sister's pushchair round the circular walk here
in gouts of rain. His last winter, we brought my dad,
shivering in his wheelchair in the carpark,
chucking the ducks' bread just anywhere.

As a child, I'd flinch when he stirred the bonfire
to make ash-flakes fly, falling sparks of paper –
witches' souls, he called them. And now my lover
has a patch of alopecia, kiss-sized, above his left ear.
But he brushes his hair secretly over it. So I forbear.
As if something scalding has touched him there.

Two cats on a Valentine's card

For one bribed instant, they sat
in a heart shape: double-tail-curled
rumps the heart's bumps,
heads close enough to bite.
You can see they don't fool
each other an inch, don't try.

This is one split-second's flicker
in a ticker tape of sniff,
cuff, hiss, hysterical arching,
pantomime affront, huff-off,
real pinching hate,
play-fight, indignant alliance.

Everyone in on this –
the animal-handler,
photographer, graphic artist,
printer, shop assistant –
knows it as cheap con, nothing
like the on and on of coupledom.

If you buy it, fool, do it
knowingly. Write *I am the cat
who walks by himself. Some nights
I choose to curl close. That's it.
You want my heart? OK. My heart's
like that.*

Salad spinner

I have failed to convey to you why
I hate it so much. You laugh. There's
something obscene in plastic things –

that the dinosaurs died, prehistoric forests
went to mush, the whole world boiled down
to an abscess of oil underground and

the present world ripped apart to get it out,
the roads stampeding through the woods,
nothing untrodden, most of it landfill

within a couple of decades, and then
the third world factories. You stand there,
turning it, tiny prim plastic wheels biting on

nothing, the world mumbled down in its gums
to get us dry lettuce. I do nothing about any of it.
It makes me want to spit when you take

the rinsed leaves from me, stand with it
under one arm like a mandolin, whirring. Worst
is that I suspect I don't even think this:

it's all wholesale from my mother,
dirty hippy, proud as a filthy old aristocrat.
This is something to do with her life thirty years ago.

I am too good for you. As you make my dinner
I blame you for everything I haven't done
since I was twenty. Stop being so considerate

with your damn salad. Let me out of this lovely
Victorian semi on the right side of town, mortgage
practically paid off, convenient for the theatre.

Let me eat pesticides. Let me eat mud.

Anniversary present

Most of the intricate and various Victorian marvels
have lost their glass domes. Some are gummed up,
or dust silts deep in their clockwork.
Their tiny pasted hairs and feathers are dim with dirt,
or they grate with rust in spots like lichen.

So it seems to me generous to be given this –
a glass like a hat, like a diving bell for a thought,
a case to guard something that's precious
because of the effort and skill
and the share of a lifetime it took to make it.

Thank you for the possibility of it. Thank you for believing
I'd find or save or construct something worthy
of being the glory inside it. For your blithe
and lovely assumption, after all these years,
that is who I am.

Anemone

Always the ones you don't want
wanting to suck your fingers
and kiss your neck. They insist
on buying you another drink.
They work out your pleasures
and use them.

It's like trying to walk
out of the sea barefoot
over tumbling stones
and the tide going out
stroking your ankles.

Statistically, it's single men,
young strapping single men
like my poor soft neighbour,
six foot four and vulnerable as hell,
who get jumped in alleyways,
roughed up and expected to take it.

Stuff like that is the trap
that makes you feel
you ought to open up
like an anemone for them –
be mother sex.
Poor men.

There is a thing

                    that's maybe me
or maybe part of me. A warm
and snouting thing that snuffles round
at possibilities, that bounds
across the fields alongside my commute,
that one day really will
abandon the train at Manningtree,
leave personal effects behind
and vanish.

The thing can sense a kindred thing
across a crowded room, can feel
potential heat in a withheld hand,
can strike a flint on the look
in a stranger's eye as he returns
my pen in smiling silence.
The thing's

quite certain of itself – it knows
these possibilities are real,
looks out from the cell
that is also maybe me
or part of me
and doesn't howl.

Tease

I know my luck
to be safe enough
to try my luck –
to flirt back

although he's bigger than me
and although I feel the fizz
of sex-tension as he sits again
too close

we are all civilised here
it's safe
to bat the entendres back
return the odd glance

but I watch my back walking home
unlock lock the door quick
slip through
double-bolt

like a matador feeling slow

Valentine, thirteen years in

for Adam

Love, I want you clothed.
I want you to yawn and stretch
so I glimpse the reach
of skin at the base of your back
under rucked fabric.
That place I feel the muscles react
when we hug. Like the sway
in the trunk of a tree
when the wind moves its branches.

Then I want you turned away
so I can slip my hands round
from behind, under your T-shirt
and cradle your belly
warm in its burrow.
So I can put my face blind
against the oak door of your back.
So anyone but me
might not be sure it's you.

NOTES ON THE POEMS

'Jill had two ponies', page 2
This poem refers to the Jill's Ponies series of books by Rub
Ferguson.

'Daphne', page 9
Wikipedia says: 'Daphne is a minor figure in Greek mytholog
known as a naiad [...] There are several versions of the myth.' I
Ovid's version, Daphne was a great beauty and a sworn virgin
The god Apollo pursued her to ravish her and Daphne was turne
into a tree to escape him.

'Marilyn', page 15
The text in italics is made up of quotes from *Breakfast at Tiffany*
by Truman Capote, *Some Like It Hot* by Billy Wilder and I.A.L
Diamond, and from newspaper interviews with Tony Curtis.

ACKNOWLEDGEMENTS

Some of these poems, or earlier versions of them, were first published in *Lighthouse, Magma, Poetry Salzburg Review, The North, The Rialto*, and *Under The Radar*.

'No Better Than She Should Be Red' was longlisted in the 2018 Rialto/RSPB Nature Poetry Competition.

ABOUT THE POET

Ramona Herdman lives in Norwich and is a committee member for Café Writers. Her pamphlet *Bottle* (HappenStance Press) was the Poetry Book Society Pamphlet Choice for Spring 2018 and one of the Poetry School's Books of the Year 2017. She won the Poetry Society's Hamish Canham prize in 2017. Her first collection, *Come what you wished for*, was published by Egg Box in 2003.

Ramona was awarded a Hawthornden Fellowship in 2019, during which this pamphlet was finalised.

ABOUT THE EMMA PRESS

The Emma Press is an independent publishing house based in the Jewellery Quarter, Birmingham, UK. It was founded in 2012 by Emma Dai'an Wright and specialises in poetry, short fiction and children's books.

The Emma Press has been shortlisted for the Michael Marks Award for Poetry Pamphlet Publishers in 2014, 2015, 2016, 2018 and 2020, winning in 2016. Moon Juice, a poetry collection by Kate Wakeling for children aged 8+, won the 2017 CLiPPA.

In 2020 The Emma Press received funding from Arts Council England's Elevate programme, developed to enhance the diversity of the arts and cultural sector by strengthening the resilience of diverse-led organisations.

The Emma Press is passionate about publishing literature which is welcoming and accessible.

Visit our website and find out more about our books here:
Website: theemmapress.com
Facebook @theemmapress
Twitter @theemmapress
Instagram @theemmapress

Lightning Source UK Ltd.
Milton Keynes UK
UKHW012252080721
386851UK00003B/141